Political and Economic Systems
DICTATORSHIP

Richard Tames

Heinemann Library
Chicago, Illinois

© 2008 Heinemann Library
a division of Reed Elsevier Inc.
Chicago, Illinois

Customer Service 888-454-2279
Visit our website at www.heinemannraintree.com

Designed by Richard Parker and Q2A Creative
Printed and bound in Hong Kong

12 11 10 09 08
10 9 8 7 6 5 4 3 2 1

New edition ISBN: 978-1-4329-0234-6 (hardcover)
                   978-1-4329-0759-4 (paperback)

**The Library of Congress has catalogued the first
edition as follows:**
Tames, Richard.
     Dictatorship / Richard Tames.
        p. cm. -- (Political and economic systems)
Summary: Discusses the history and theory behind
dictatorship as a political system and explains how it has been applied in practice.
Includes bibliographical references and index.
     ISBN 1-40340-318-X
     1. Dictatorship -- Juvenile literature. [1. Dictatorship] I. Title. II. Series.
     JC495 .T36 2003
     321.9--dc21

                              2002006315

Acknowledgments
The publishers would like to thank the following for permission to reproduce photographs:
Bridgeman: p. 25; Bridgeman/British Museum: p. 17; Corbis/Archivo Iconografico: pp. 16, 24;
Corbis/Bettmann: pp. 20, 28, 32, 40, 42; Corbis/Bill Gentile: p. 11; Corbis/Charles Lenars: p.
16; Corbis/Christel Gerstenberg: p. 35; Corbis/Sygma: p. 53; Corbis/Sygma/Robert Patrick: p.
50; Empics/AP p. 48; Getty Images/Hulton: pp. 6, 8, 26, 31, 37; Kobal Collection: p. 21; Rex:
p. 45.

Cover photograph of a statue of Soviet leader Joseph Stalin reproduced with permission of
Getty Images/Time Life Pictures/Chris Niedenthal. Background image reproduced with
permission of istockphoto.com/Kristen Johansen

Our thanks to Christopher Gibb and Stewart Ross for their comments in the preparation of
this book.

Contents

Any words appearing in the text in bold, **like this**, are explained in the glossary.

The Night of the Long Knives

On June 29, 1934, dozens of tough-looking men wearing brown uniform shirts gathered from all over Germany at a hotel in the lakeside resort of Bad Wiesee. Respectable Germans disliked them as rowdy bullies, but they were also afraid of them. They were members of the **SA—Sturmabteilung** (Storm Troopers)—the **Nazi** party's **militia**. The Nazi party under Adolf Hitler had been the government of Germany since January 1933. SA men strutted the streets, drilled and practiced with weapons and looked forward to even more power in the new Nazi Germany.

The SA's top commander, Ernst Röhm, had launched Hitler's political career. He was confident of Hitler's support for his plan to absorb the regular German army into the SA, with himself in command. Röhm could not have been more wrong. Hitler saw the SA as too big and dangerously out of his direct control. He now wanted to work with the professional armed forces to rearm Germany, and to win the support of respectable Germans in making the country prosperous again.

Hitler arrived unexpectedly early at Bad Wiesee on the morning of June 30, 1934. Röhm and the other top SA leaders were still asleep. They were immediately disarmed, arrested, and taken away by Hitler's personal bodyguard, black-uniformed **SS—Schutzstaffel** (defense squadron) men, to Nazi party headquarters in Munich, where they were shot. There were other executions without trial throughout the country. Not all of the victims were SA men. Others were political opponents that Hitler decided to get rid of in the same operation.

It was announced that Röhm had been planning to seize power for himself, and the government admitted that 87 plotters had been killed. The real number was probably hundreds. Newspapers were forbidden to publish details of the victims and all documents connected with the measures taken on June 30, and July 1 and 2 were destroyed, so no one could be sure. On July 4, at a special ceremony, Hitler personally presented each SS executioner with a special dagger to honor their loyalty to him. On July 13 he told the German Reichstag (parliament), "If any one ... asks why I did not turn to the regular courts ... then all I can say to him is this: in this hour I was responsible for the fate of the German people and thereby I became the supreme judge on behalf of the German people ... I gave the orders to shoot the ringleaders in this treason ..."

Leaders of the world's **democracies** were as horrified to hear Hitler's claim that he stood above the law as they were at his open use of murder. But among ordinary German people there was widespread approval. They believed the fake evidence of a plot and applauded Hitler's merciless action against the alleged plotters. Germany's generals were pleased to see SA plans to take over the military ended. Germany's leading law professor, Carl Schmitt of Berlin University, praised Hitler's direct justice.

Less than a month later, Germany's aged president, Paul von Hindenburg, died. Hitler then simply merged the vacant position of president with his own post of chancellor (prime minister) and made himself commander-in-chief as well, with the single title of Führer (leader). All officers, soldiers, and government officials from then on were made to swear a personal oath of loyalty and obedience to Adolf Hitler, the Führer of the German Reich and German People. Hitler had shown that even those who thought they were his loyal supporters were not safe from his **arbitrary** power. He had taken one more decisive step towards making himself dictator— sole master—of Europe's largest nation.

Forms of **dictatorship** can be traced back to ancient Greece, but Adolf Hitler ranks with Joseph Stalin of the **Soviet Union** and Mao Zedong of China as examples of the new type of dictator made possible by technology in the 20th century.

The styles of government they created are known as **totalitarian** because they wanted total control over the people they governed. No aspect of people's lives—the friends they had, what they read, how they spent their free time—was considered to be a purely private matter, outside politics. Dictators have always wanted to crush opposition to their rule. In modern times they also tried to transform the country they governed.

Hitler at the microphone. He spent many hours rehearsing his speeches and the dramatic gestures that accompanied them.

Sayings of the dictators

Adolf Hitler
"I learned the use of terror from the communists, of slogans from the Catholic church, and the use of **propaganda** from the democracies."
"The greater the lie, the greater the chance it will be believed."
"With us the Leader and the Idea are one and every party member has to do what the leader orders."
"In starting and waging a war it is not right that matters, but victory."

Joseph Stalin
"We are fifty or a hundred years behind the advanced countries. We must make good this distance within ten years. Either we do it or they crush us."
"A single death is a tragedy: a million is a statistic."

Mao Zedong
"Political power grows out of the barrel of a gun."
"A revolution is not a dinner party or writing an essay or doing embroidery. A revolution is an act of violence ..."

What Makes a Dictatorship?

Adolf Hitler's ruthless treatment of his own supporters on the Night of the Long Knives shows a number of the key features of a modern dictatorship.

Concentration of power

Decision making is in the hands of either a single dictator or a small committee. There are no legal checks and balances against their abuse of power, except the failure of the system to act efficiently. This can happen when the dictator rewards loyal followers with jobs that they are too corrupt or incompetent to carry out, or when they work against each other to increase their personal power.

Arbitrary rule

The **constitution**, if there is one, is largely meaningless in practice. Laws are either ignored or misapplied. There is no effective **rule of law**. **Secret police** operate outside the law to spy on and destroy all opposition. Dictatorships readily and routinely use violence to repress opposition by imprisoning or murdering their opponents or driving them into **exile**. But dictatorships cannot be based on violence and repression alone. At the very least they need the obedience of the police, armed forces, or party **militia** to use violence against their opponents.

A ruling ideology

An **ideology** is a set of ideas that defines a political system. Democracies tolerate differing ideas about both the methods and goals of politics, but dictatorships force people to accept a single ideology. This is the officially approved view of what political action should achieve and what methods should be used to achieve it. Other goals and methods are suppressed. The main instrument for imposing an ideology is usually a political party led by the dictator. Normally it is the only allowed party, but is often supported by other organizations, such as militias, youth movements, and women's groups.

Core supporters

Winning the active support of at least part of the general population limits the need for violence and is essential for stability. Depending on the country concerned, important groups of supporters might include landowners, trade unions, tribal chiefs, students, or religious institutions.

In the 20th century, dictatorships usually wanted much more than mere obedience. They tried to get the majority of the population involved in carrying out political programs, such as redistributing land, building up industry, or expanding the armed forces.

Successful dictatorships recruited positive supporters to serve as party officials, militia officers and so on, and rewarded them with high-paying jobs and influence in the system. They also gained more passive, less committed support from groups that benefited from their rule. These benefits might be material, such as land, jobs, healthcare, or education, or they might be psychological, like pride in one's country or race,

Mussolini in Fascist Party uniform hails an adoring crowd. Many dictatorships have been genuinely popular and needed little force to keep their power. Mussolini's rousing speeches excited and flattered his followers into believing they were building a great new future for Italy.

expulsion of a foreign ruler, overthrow of a cruel government, defeat of a hated enemy, or order and stability after a period of chaos.

Throughout the 20th century, democracy and dictatorship were rivals as systems of government. Perhaps surprisingly, democracy seemed to win this rivalry. This did not look likely in Europe in the 1930s, when **fascism** was on the rise, or after World War II, when **communism** was spreading through every continent, or in the 1970s, when many newly independent countries in Asia and Africa lurched between dictatorship and chaos. Fascism was crushed by defeat in World War II. With the breakup of the **Soviet Union** in 1989-1991, communism collapsed there and in eastern Europe, and was weakened in the rest of the world. Throughout Asia, Africa, and Latin America dictatorships have given in to democracies, although that trend has been uneven and sometimes reversed.

Explaining their politics

Fascism
"Fascism is a religion: the 20th century will be known as the century of fascism."
"For the fascist, everything is in the state and nothing human or spiritual exists, much less has value, outside the state."
"Fascism believes that permanent peace is neither possible nor useful."
Benito Mussolini

"A creed entirely given over to hate, to irreverence, and to violence." Pope Pius XI

Nazism
"We must develop organizations in which an individual's entire life can take place. Then every activity and every need of every individual will be regulated ... by the party ... there are no longer any free realms in which the individual belongs to himself ... The time of personal happiness is over." Adolf Hitler

Communism
"The theory of communism may be summed up in one sentence : Abolish all private property." Karl Marx and Friedrich Engels
"Communism has nothing to do with love. It is an excellent hammer which we use to destroy our enemy." Mao Zedong

Styles of Dictatorship

Many dictatorships showed the outward trappings of democratic government—a **constitution**, elections, newspapers, even **demonstrations**. But in a dictatorship these do not affect how the political system actually works—because of corruption, force, fraud, terror, and trickery.

Democracies have a more or less family resemblance to one another. They are based either on some variation of the American or French presidential **republics** or on the British Westminster model of parliamentary government. Dictatorships, by contrast, developed in many forms, though often borrowing techniques of government from one another.

The fascist **regimes** of Italy (1922–1943) and Germany (1933–1945) and their imitators and allies before and during World War II were based on the idea of an inspired Man of Destiny, who could transform his nation by winning the eager, disciplined support of the people.

The *caudillismo* of Latin America and Spain continued the 19th-century traditions of the rule of a strong man. *Caudillos* were supported by the armed forces and by the Roman Catholic church in the interests of order and stability. Sometimes they borrowed the outward style of fascism, in such things as party uniforms, **propaganda**, youth movements, and mass rallies, but they usually tried to keep things as they were rather than make great changes.

In 1973 Argentina's former dictator, Juan Péron, returned from exile to be freely elected as president but he died the following year after failing to tackle the country's economic problems. In 1976 the military seized power, banned all political parties, and carried on a Dirty War against any opponents who dared to challenge its rule. About 15,000 people disappeared and must be presumed dead. In 1982, to distract Argentines from their problems, the **junta** leader General Galtieri ordered the invasion of the British-occupied Falkland Islands, which Argentina had long claimed as its own.

For more information on Péron and Pinochet, see pages 59–60.

For a few weeks the military was popular, but when Britain recaptured the islands Galtieri was forced from power and civilian rule was restored.

Communist states theoretically tried to free the mass of ordinary people and offer them a better life in a more just society. In practice they repressed them through the use of **secret police**, militias, and party and state officials. Sometimes dictatorial power in communist states was in the hands of

Chilean military dictator Augusto Pinochet (with sash) reviews a military parade. Starting in the 1960s, a new form of dictatorship emerged in Latin America, in which senior officers, supported by well-disciplined and established armed forces and aided by **technocrats**, seized power to solve an economic crisis or crush extremist movements.

committees of party officials, sometimes power was exercised by a single individual. Some communist states lasted for half a century or more. Others, like Colonel Haile Mariam Mengistu's in Ethiopia (1977–91), called themselves communist but failed to establish lasting regimes because of the strain of constant war.

Africa and Asia created a wide range of regimes in former European **colonies** that gained independence starting in the 1940s. They varied greatly in what they claimed to represent and in the degree of bloodshed and chaos they caused. Two main types of dictatorship emerged.

The first was the **civilian** system. This was based on a single ruling political party, headed by a **charismatic** politician, often the leader of the movement for national independence. A good example was Kwame Nkrumah (1909–1972), ruler of Ghana from its independence in 1957 to his overthrow by the army in 1966.

The second type of dictatorship was the military regime. This was based on newly established armed forces and often led by a junior, or at least a newly promoted and inexperienced officer, such as Idi Amin, dictator of Uganda from 1971 to 1979.

Both types of dictatorship were often split by conflicts between different tribes, regions, or ethnic or religious groups. Both tended to become purely personal systems of rule, which proved incapable either of delivering effective government or of building strong regimes that would outlast the dictator himself. These systems of personal rule might genuinely try to turn a political vision into reality, such as transforming a poor agricultural country into a modern industrial one. But many simply became robber regimes, treating the state as the private property of the dictator, to be used for his personal benefit and to buy the loyalty of such people as favored generals, party bosses, and business leaders.

Dictators and monarchs

Although dictatorship was known in the ancient world, it only became common starting in the 19th century. For most of human history states have been governed by **monarchs**—with titles such as king, tsar or czar, shah, sultan, rajah, or emperor. Unlike modern dictators, monarchs rarely based their claim to rule on their personality or the need to carry out a political program. Normally a king had to be of royal blood. He was usually the son or brother of the previous ruler or at least chosen by him, and was often confirmed in office by a coronation ceremony or some form of acceptance by a council of powerful nobles or priests. Although some kings did act like modern dictators in ruling by terror or ordering the killing of their opponents, most accepted limits to their power. These were usually set by law, custom, or religion. Kings acknowledged that even they were subject or answerable to some higher power, usually divine. Unlike kings, who usually inherit their position, dictators justify their right to rule by claiming to be extraordinary men or promising to do extraordinary things.

A bust of the young Roman emperor Caligula (ruled CE 37–41). Occasionally, traditional monarchs behaved as arbitrarily as modern dictators. Rulers whose cruelty seemed totally arbitrary, like the Roman emperors Caligula or Commodus (ruled CE 180–192)—both of whom came to believe that they were gods—usually ended up being murdered, often by their own bodyguards.

Machiavelli—principles or power ?

Beginning in the 14th century, Italy started to resemble ancient Greece because it was divided into contending city-states that were frequently at war with one another. Some were ruled by princes. Others were republics in form, but were ruled in practice by the head of a powerful family who was a prince in everything except actual name. Florence was run by the fabulously rich Medici family for three centuries. They became celebrated as generous patrons of poets and painters, who in return were expected to glorify the Medici.

These princely rulers were known as **despots**. Like modern dictators, they wanted to concentrate power in their own hands and were constantly on guard against rivals, whom they were prepared to imprison or even murder. Like modern dictators, they often claimed to be ruling for the benefit of their people and justified their personal power by saying that it was necessary to guard against foreign enemies. Unlike modern dictators, however, they had no ambition to control the lives of their subjects in detail, providing they were content to stay out of politics. Moreover, unlike many modern dictators, they at least pretended to respect the official religion of the state.

Beginning in the Middle Ages, many European handbooks were written to tell rulers how to govern. Almost all were written by leaders in the church, who naturally declared that rulers should follow the teachings of the Church and be truthful, generous, fair, and merciful. *The Prince*, a brutally realistic work written by Niccolo Machiavelli (1469–1527) in 1513, was quite different. Machiavelli had worked for the republican government of Florence until it was overthrown in 1512. He lost his job and used his forced retirement to write about what he had learned. Machiavelli knew from firsthand experience that real Italian politics was full of blackmail, betrayal, and murder. His starting point was his own rather low opinion of human nature, "One can make this generalization about men: they are ungrateful, fickle, liars and deceivers, they avoid danger and are greedy for profit ..."

Machiavelli wrote at a time when Italy had become a battleground for invading French and Spanish armies. As an Italian who wanted to see the foreigners driven out and order restored, Machiavelli hoped that a strong and ruthless leader would emerge to do the job. The main purpose of *The Prince* was to show such a man how to gain power and, having gained power, how to use it and keep it. The most important quality a ruler needed was what Machiavelli called *virtu*, which can be translated as "guts" or "nerve"—the willingness to do what needs to be done in an uncertain world of unseen threats, sudden dangers, and unpredictable crises.

Machiavelli warned rulers against enjoying cruelty and advised them to make their subjects prosperous and happy. He knew that those with power inevitably have enemies, so it is foolish to add to their number without good cause. But when it was essential to act there should be no holding back, "The injury done to a man ought to be such that you do not need to fear his revenge."

Machiavelli knew that rulers were faced with life and death decisions that ordinary citizens did not face. Therefore, to stay in power, they had to do things which would be very wrong for

Models for Machiavelli

Some scholars believe that Machiavelli had the career of Cosimo de Medici (1389–1464) in mind when he was writing about the perfect prince. Cosimo used a fortune made from banking to bribe his way to power in Florence. He kept up the pretense that it was a republic, but packed all positions of power with his trusted supporters who constantly renewed his right to rule as a dictator. In theory his powers were purely temporary, but in practice they were permanent. Cosimo also used his money to hire troops from the Sforza family of Milan, thus freeing himself from the need to keep the Florentines personally loyal. Cosimo ruled Florence from 1434 until his death. The Medicis ruled Florence almost continuously until 1737.

Machiavelli also certainly knew and admired Cesare Borgia (1475–1507), the illegitimate son of Pope Alexander VI, who made Borgia an archbishop when he was only seventeen. A brilliant lawyer, Cesare proved an equally outstanding commander of the Pope's army, conquering large parts of central Italy. He had his own brother-in-law murdered and executed army commanders who plotted against him, but he lost his power when his father died, probably from poison.

a private individual because, "Politics have no relation to morals." But Machiavelli also realized that appearance and reality are two different things and a prince should try at least to look like a good man. "He should appear to be merciful, faithful to his word, kind, straightforward and religious ... But his character should be such that if he needs to be the opposite he knows how ... a prince, and especially a new prince, cannot observe all those things which give men a reputation for virtue, because in order to defend his state he is often forced to act against good faith, kindness, charity, or religion ... so he should be flexible ..., he should not depart from what is good, if that is possible, but he should know how to do evil, if that is necessary."

Machiavelli's frankness made his name a byword for wickedness. Deceit, betrayal, plotting, and assassination came to be denounced as Machiavellian. Some thinkers, however, believed that Machiavelli should be praised for writing about politics as it really is, not as it should be.

Niccolo Machiavelli, the 16th-century Italian philosopher whose book *The Prince* was a handbook for politicians without principles.

The possibilities of power

The power of traditional monarchies to interfere with the lives of their ordinary subjects depended on the resources and technologies they could command. Only the richest rulers had permanent armies. Most had to rely on forces supplied by powerful nobles or subject peoples, either of whom might revolt if treated poorly. Travel was usually difficult and often dangerous. Warfare was largely seasonal, rarely happening in winter. Politics concerned only a tiny elite. The mass of the population was unquestioningly loyal to the king unless actually driven to revolt. Nobody liked paying the taxes that the king used to pay his soldiers, judges, and officials but most people valued a strong monarchy to defend them from invaders and punish criminals.

Traditional monarchies were supported by religious ideologies. Christianity, Islam, and Buddhism all taught that the world was ordered by a divine power, represented on earth by rulers who governed righteously if they upheld religion and its teachings. Obedience to religion in this life would be rewarded in the afterlife.

Modern dictators are far less limited than traditional monarchs. Industrialization has greatly increased the wealth available to governments to create mass **literacy** and employ large numbers of officials, armed forces, and police. Sophisticated technology, ranging from the simple typewriter and telephone to electronic surveillance and digital record-keeping, have made it possible to regulate and control in detail the lives of the majority of citizens.

In some parts of the world the decline in religious belief has removed a traditional check on a ruler's powers. Those with no belief in life after death may be more willing to follow a leader who promises them power and prosperity in their life on Earth. Modern ideologies, such as communism and fascism, look to the future but claim to transform life now for the better. Communist dictatorships tried to destroy the power of organized religion. They closed churches, seized church property, imprisoned priests, and used the school system to attack religious beliefs. The Nazis treated Christianity as though it was out of date and irrelevant. They even tried to develop a **pagan** alternative, based on ancient German gods and legends. In fascist Italy, where the Roman Catholic Church was too powerful to ignore, Mussolini used its

Allah's will

In the Islamic world some governments base their right to rule on the claim that they are enforcing Allah's laws.

In 1979 the rule of the shah (king) of Iran was overthrown by a mass movement led by the country's religious leaders. The Islamic republic they created has an elected parliament, but all laws, appointments, and government decisions may be overturned by the country's religious dictators: the Supreme Leader and the Guardian Council appointed by him.

Saudi Arabia is a monarchy, but claims to have no constitution except the Qur'an, the holy scripture of Islam. The king, guided by his family and religious experts, rules by decree although recently local elections have been permitted.

Dictators cannot accept that they are ever wrong about anything. Religious fanatics have the same mindset and can easily become dictators. This is what happened in Afghanistan after an extreme Islamic group known as the Taliban spearheaded the defeat of invading Russians. The Taliban took over the government and from 1994 to 2001 exercised a religious dictatorship over the country. Men had to wear beards, TV and all forms of non-Islamic art and culture were banned, and women lost all rights. With massive U.S. support, the Taliban were overthrown in 2001–02.

fear of communism to limit its criticisms of his rule. On the whole, the church accepted fascism as better than chaos or communism.

New technologies

New technologies have given dictators the power to use violence on a whole new scale. In the past, mobs of rebellious peasants armed with farmyard tools often defeated regular soldiers, at least for a while, but would be easily **massacred** by professional troops with armored vehicles and rapid-firing weapons. Ivan the Terrible ruled Russia brutally from 1547–84 and was responsible for killing thousands who rebelled against his rule. But he could only enforce his will through men riding on horses, armed with swords and primitive guns.

A portrait of Ivan the Terrible. Comparatively few of his subjects would have known what he looked like during his reign—this impression of him was painted by the Russian artist Viktor Vasnetsov nearly 350 years later.

Joseph Stalin, dictator of the Soviet Union from 1928 to 1953, used police forces and militias with machine guns and artillery, trucks and tanks and railways, to wipe out millions of peasants who opposed his land reforms. He did this either by mass murder or he created famines by cutting off food supplies to entire regions.

New technologies of communication have brought the rulers and the ruled much closer together. Cheap printing, photography, radio, film, TV, and the Internet have enabled rulers to communicate directly with their people. For example, most subjects of Russia's Ivan the Terrible had no idea what he looked like, whereas Soviet citizens saw the face of dictator Stalin everywhere, in newspapers and magazines, on posters and in school textbooks. Every town had a statue of him. Every year tens of thousands of people marched in great parades in front of him in person, but tens of millions could feel part of these events thanks to radio and movie theater newsreels.

Stalin's purges

Lenin's death in 1924 was followed by a power struggle from which Stalin emerged as victor by 1928. He then introduced a series of Five Year Plans intended to transform the USSR into a modern industrial nation and bring all farming under state control. By simply taking land from the richer peasants (*kulaks*) and confiscating grain from the rest, Stalin caused a famine that killed more than six million people.

In 1934 Stalin ordered the murder of Sergei Kirov, a local communist leader in Leningrad whose popularity he took as a threat to his own position. Kirov's death was then used as a pretext for the arrest and trial of hundreds and then thousands of loyal communists on trumped up charges of terrorism, plotting or sabotaging industry. The purge of suspected traitors was then extended to the armed forces, leading to the execution or imprisonment of 35,000 officers. By 1938 about 8 million people had been arrested and just under 7 million people had been sent to camps as slave labor to build roads, dams, factories, and power supplies. Less than 3 percent survived the standard ten year sentence. When Stalin died in 1953, there were still 12 million prisoners in labor camps.

A nightmare vision

The English **socialist** George Orwell (1903–50) wrote his novel *Nineteen Eighty-Four* immediately after World War II, when the full horrors of **Nazism** were being revealed and the communist USSR, under Stalin, was taking over the former democracies of eastern Europe.

In *Nineteen Eighty-Four*, the world is divided into three empires, constantly at war with each other. The permanent crisis of war enables the Party, headed by Big Brother, to justify its complete power by claiming ever-present dangers from traitors and enemies that require the constant use of torture and terror. Every home is fitted with video screens so the government can spy on everyone all the time. Children are rewarded for betraying their parents to the Thought Police if they say anything against the Party or Big Brother. There is no right to privacy, there is no such thing as private life, there are no rights. Everyone must dedicate their life to the Party and positively love Big Brother.

The hero of *Nineteen Eighty-Four*, Winston Smith, is a victim of the system that oppresses him and everyone else outside the leadership of the Party. He is employed at the Ministry of Truth, constantly rewriting history so that no one can challenge the Party's complete control of information. This control is strengthened by the spread of Newspeak, a deliberately simplified form of English designed to end free thought by destroying the power to make contrasts or distinctions. In Newspeak, the words wrong, illegal, immoral, wicked and evil are replaced by the all-purpose term doubleplusungood.

When Winston Smith falls in love, he challenges the entire system and must pay the price. He is tortured until he will agree that two plus two makes five and believes that they do so, until he will not only obey the Party but actually loves Big Brother—and does so sincerely.

An image from a film version of *Nineteen Eighty-Four* made in 1984. The book was written as a warning, rather than a prophecy, a picture of what could happen, not what inevitably would.

21

The Origins of Dictatorship

Dictatorship is essentially a modern form of government, but it has had forerunners in the past that have inspired some of its forms and features. Modern dictators have sometimes been inspired by the example of great historical figures of the ancient world, like Julius Caesar, or military adventurers like Genghis Khan and Napoleon Bonaparte.

Ancient Greece

Greek thinkers recognized an oppressive form of one-man rule. They called it **tyranny**. The tyrant either ignored the law and seized power by force, or inherited his position from someone who had. Because tyranny usually rested on the personal qualities of the tyrant—ambition, toughness, military skill, courage, ruthlessness—tyrannical rule often ended with the death of the tyrant or the overthrow of a successor too weak to hang on to power. Tyranny therefore was considered to be a form of rule that was basically unstable.

Tyrants were also installed by foreign powers, such as Persia and Macedonia, to rule conquered Greek city-states on their behalf. These tyrannies could last longer because the power of the tyrant depended less on personal qualities than on the use of foreign troops to suppress opposition.

Greek thinkers saw that in some situations tyranny might have value, such as bringing order after war or helping to make the transition from rule by a small aristocracy to a more democratic form of government. Individual tyrants were sometimes great builders or generous patrons of artists and poets. But more often tyrants abused their power and acted cruelly, so the Greeks generally came to disapprove of tyranny.

Rome

Dictatorship in the early Roman republic was almost the opposite of what it became in the 20th century. It arose from emergency situations, such as the need to suppress a rebellion, but it was a legal position, intended to last for only a limited time.

The dictator was given complete power by the senate, Rome's supreme lawmaking body, but only for a maximum of six months. Any abuse of power might be punished afterward by the law.

The ambitious Roman general Sulla (138–78 BCE) was appointed dictator in 82 BCE after a civil war and used his power to have dozens of political opponents murdered. By packing the senate with his supporters, he got it to declare his actions legal. This later inspired another ambitious general, Julius Caesar (c.102–44 BCE). He was also appointed dictator after a civil war and then dictator for life. When he had his image stamped on the coinage, like a king, members of the old aristocracy that controlled the senate saw that he was turning his position into a monarchy. They murdered him to preserve the republic, thus starting another, even worse, civil war that destroyed republican government completely.

France—crises in contrast

In the early stages of the French Revolution, when a republic had just been established, it was threatened by anti-revolutionary armies of exiles along its borders. Thousands of prisoners, accused of being enemies of the revolution in France, were massacred without trial. The revolutionary government came under the control of a fanatical lawyer, Maximilien Robespierre (1758–94). Like a Roman dictator defending the state in an hour of crisis, he continued the Reign of Terror until French victories ended the crisis.

In 1958 the French Fourth Republic collapsed over the future of Algeria, a French **colony** fighting for its independence. Party leaders appealed to retired war hero General Charles de Gaulle (1890–1970), liberator of France from Nazi occupation, restorer of democracy and, briefly, first post-war head of government. As a man above politics, he was asked to take power and rescue France from the risk of a military coup or even civil war. De Gaulle used his position to draw up a **constitution** for a new Fifth Republic with greatly strengthened powers for the President, a position de Gaulle himself held until 1969. He thus played the role of a Roman-style dictator, using temporary powers to reestablish constitutional government, rather than to end it.

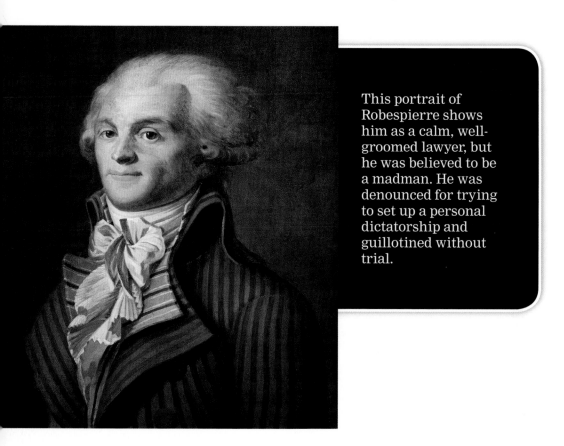

This portrait of Robespierre shows him as a calm, well-groomed lawyer, but he was believed to be a madman. He was denounced for trying to set up a personal dictatorship and guillotined without trial.

Soldiers of fortune

In medieval Europe successful kings were warriors, usually commanding the army in person. Most nobles were trained as fighting men and peasants were expected to defend their homes. During the 16th century, full-time professional armies came into being. This created the possibility that an ambitious general could use his army to seize power for himself.

Oliver Cromwell (1599–1658), reluctant dictator

In the mid-16th century, civil war, the execution of Charles I, and the abolition of the monarchy left England in a state of confusion. In an attempt the produce stability and fair government, the military commander Oliver Cromwell took over the government. He refused the offer of the crown, but did live in a palace, had his image stamped on the coinage and took the title Lord Protector of the Commonwealth. Cromwell's conquests brought the entire British Isles under one ruler for the first time, but he failed to provide for a successor. On his deathbed Cromwell chose his son Richard to succeed him, but Tumbledown Dick (as he was nicknamed) had been kept out of politics and was just ignored. Another former general, George Monck (1608–70), arranged to restore the monarchy and was royally rewarded for it. Cromwell's rule, unique in English history, had been efficient and well-meaning and he was nicknamed the Reluctant Dictator.

This portrait shows Cromwell as a royal figure, much like the king he had executed. Cromwell was an unambitious English country gentleman until civil war (1642–49) showed his unexpected talent as a commander in the victorious Parliamentary army.

Napoleon Bonaparte (1769–1821)

Unlike Cromwell, Napoleon was a professional soldier from his youth. He was also intensely ambitious. His military brilliance and the extraordinary opportunities created by the French Revolution made him an army commander at the age of just 26. Napoleon soon turned military glory into political power by becoming first a member of the government, then leader of the government for life, then crowning himself emperor (1804). As emperor he gave France the code of laws still in force today and conquered most of Europe before being finally defeated and dying in exile, a prisoner of the British.

Napoleon's extraordinary career inspired his nephew, Louis-Napoleon (Napoleon III, 1808–73) to a life of conspiracy and exile until he, too, managed to come to power in a French republic. He imitated his uncle by overthrowing the republic to put himself on the throne of a Second Empire (1852–70). This, too, was crushed by military defeat by Prussia in 1870, and Napoleon III died in exile in Britain.

Caudillismo

Simon Bolivar (1783–1830) was dictator successively of Venezuela, Colombia, and Peru. He tried to give each country a republican government. He failed in his hope of bringing all the Spanish-speaking states of the region into a single unit along the lines of the United States. Bolivia, formerly Upper Peru, became a separate state, named in his honor.

An idealized portrait of Simon Bolivar shows him as a fearless and inspiring frontline commander. Noble by birth and a lawyer by training, Bolivar led the armies that freed the colonies of South America from Spanish rule.

Bolivar's career inspired many imitators, most of them with far less noble motives. In the 1820s the newly independent countries of Latin America were in much the same position as **post-colonial** states in Africa in the 1960s—rich in resources, but poor in educated manpower. National unity was held back by poor communications and ethnic divisions.

Many countries fell under the rule of *caudillos*. Some controlled a whole country, others only a region—but in Latin America a region might be as big as Belgium or Denmark. In many cases the *caudillos* relied on private armies, recruited from the peasants who worked their large estates, to enforce their will. Juan Manuel de Rosas (1793–1877) raised a private army to seize power in Argentina, ruling by terror until his overthrow (1852). He then escaped to exile in England. In Paraguay, Francisco Solano López (1827–70) modeled himself after Napoleon and provoked a catastrophic five-year war against Brazil, Uruguay, and Argentina. It took Paraguay two generations to recover from it.

Full-scale wars between countries were relatively rare in Latin America, so in many countries the underemployed military were tempted to interfere in politics. Once established, the pattern of change of government by *golpe* (coup) and rule by a *junta* (council) of military commanders, occurred repeatedly. Since winning independence from Spain in 1825, Bolivia has had more than sixty revolutions and eleven constitutions. Chile and Uruguay were unusual in developing as stable republics controlled by **civilian** politicians, changing power through peaceful elections.

Offspring of war

In terms of world politics, 19th-century Latin America was a blind alley. It was largely isolated from the rest of the world and mostly free from foreign interference. In the 20th century, improved communications increased dramatically the links between states and regions. Countries trade with partners on opposite sides of the world. Large armed forces can now operate thousands of miles from their home bases since they can be transported instantaneously. The result has been a growing instability that has often destroyed political systems, opening the way to dictatorships.

World War I (1914–1918) destroyed the empires of Russia, Germany, Austria-Hungary, and Ottoman Turkey. War and economic depression led to the rise of communism in Russia, fascism in Germany and Italy, and the dictatorship of General Franco (1939–1975) in Spain. These regimes had various puppets and imitators in World War II.

World War II enabled the USSR to install communist dictatorships throughout eastern Europe. Enver Hoxha (1908–1985) of Albania and Marshal Josip Tito (1892–1980) of Yugoslavia used their anti-fascist **partisan** armies to set up communist dictatorships after the war.

For details on Mao and some other dictators, see pages 59-60.

Mao Zedong proclaims the establishment of the People's Republic of China in 1949. China then helped communists come to power in North Korea and North Vietnam.

By weakening the overseas empires of Britain, France, and the Netherlands, World War II hastened the independence of their **colonies**. Some governments of the newly-independent ex-colonies were corrupt and unable to control ethnic, religious, or tribal rivalries. Further problems arose because the economies of the new states often depended on the unreliable prices of the few crops or minerals they produced. In these difficult circumstances, ruthless yet **charismatic** leaders gained power by promising their people a better future.

A world apart

Albania's mountainous landscape hinders communications. This enabled its people to defeat invasion by Fascist Italy and helped Enver Hoxha to cut them off from the outside world.

Hoxha rose to power in the Albanian National Liberation Movement, formed with the aid of Tito's Yugoslav partisans. Declaring Albania a People's Republic in 1946, Hoxha made himself prime minister, foreign minister, defense minister and head of the Communist Party. His government took control of all farming and industry and banned both Christianity and Islam to make Albania the world's only officially atheist state.

Taking aid from the USSR and then China, Hoxha eventually criticized both for not being communist enough, leaving Albania isolated even in the communist world. In 1973, 1974, 1975, and 1982 Hoxha had alleged enemies within the government and Albanian Communist Party removed from power and imprisoned or shot. Albania meanwhile became Europe's poorest country.

Communist control broke down after Hoxha's death in 1985, leading to widespread crime, food shortages, and large-scale unemployment, worsened by an influx of ethnic Albanian refugees from neighbouring Kosovo. Thousands of Albanians have since fled abroad in search of a better life, while unstable governments at home struggle to undo the damage of half a century's isolation.

How dictatorships are justified

No dictatorship—personal or collective—openly admits to holding power for the benefit of the rulers rather than the ruled. Common justifications for dictatorship include:

- Restoring order in a country torn by riots and strikes, for example General Primo de Rivera in Spain in 1923 or General Pinochet in Chile in 1973. Primo de Rivera lost the support of the army and fell from power in 1930, opening the way to further disorder and then civil war from 1936 to 1939. Pinochet allowed Chile to return to democracy in 1989.
- The alleged breakdown of a constitution, for example the military takeover in Burma in 1962. The army has ruled Burma ever since, refusing to recognize the results of an election held in 1990, in which a civilian, democratic party won a two-thirds majority.
- The incompetence or oppression of a leader, for example the overthrow in 1966 of Ahmed Sukarno, Indonesia's independence leader, by General Suharto. Suharto's hugely corrupt regime was even worse, wasting Indonesia's natural riches on a massive scale until popular unrest forced him to resign in 1998.
- Defending a successful revolution, for example the permanent rule of the Institutional Revolutionary Party (PRI) in Mexico from the 1920s until 1997.
- Ending foreign business influence over the economy, for example the rule of Colonel Juan Péron in Argentina in the 1950s. Péron was driven into exile but returned for a second, unsuccessful term of office as elected president in 1973–74.
- Cleaning up financial corruption, for example numerous military takeovers in Nigeria. In Ghana Flight Lieutenant Jerry Rawlings seized power for this purpose in 1979 and 1981 and actually did make government more honest. He was reelected President in free elections in 1992 and 1996.
- Ending alleged political corruption, for example General Zia ul-Haq's overthrow of the civilian government of Zulfikar Ali Bhutto in Pakistan in 1977. Zia ruled until his death in 1988. Bhutto's daughter, Benazir, was twice elected prime minister until she, too, was disgraced by corruption, though this time it was financial, rather than political. The military, led by General Pervez Musharaff, seized power again in 1999.
- The promise of a better tomorrow for every citizen in return for discipline, effort, and sacrifice now. This is the most widely used justification of all, and was employed by most communist regimes, states such as Syria under Hafez al-Assad (1930–2000), as well as Iraq under Saddam Hussein (1937–2006) or Ghana under Kwame Nkrumah. These states claimed to be building a socialist society that would provide for the welfare of all its citizens.

Fascism and Its Friends

Mussolini's Italy

Italy was on the winning side in World War I but gained little from it in return for huge losses and expense. Thousands of ex-soldiers felt betrayed and resentful. A newly-founded communist party called for revolution. Benito Mussolini (1883–1945), a war veteran and journalist, recruited *Fasci di Combattimenti* (bands of fighters) to tackle the communists. Mussolini claimed to know how history was unfolding and promised that under his guidance Italy would move forward to a glorious future.

A march-past of the Italian fascist youth movement, wearing the party's black-shirt uniform. Students, like the unemployed and many ex-servicemen, found that the fascist movement offered them camaraderie and a sense of purpose lacking in civilian life.

The years after World War I saw violent **demonstrations**, organized street-fighting between fascists and communists, and the disruption of daily life by repeated strikes. The fear of revolution created a situation in which many longed for the restoration of order, even at the cost of democratic freedoms.

Mussolini claimed to have seized power by force as a result of a March on Rome in 1922, but this was a myth that suited his image as a strong man. In fact, he became prime minister of Italy quite legally, at the invitation of King Victor Emmanuel III. Mussolini's dictatorship was achieved over several years. Gradually the fascist party gained full power over politics and the media, replacing parliament with a Chamber of Corporations. This was supposed to represent groups such as labor, farmers, and intellectuals, and by doing so to have

Mussolini poses for a bust of himself as a grim-faced hero.

overcome traditional conflicts between employers and workers in the interest of the nation as a whole. Fascist posters proclaimed *Mussolini ha sempre ragione* (Mussolini is always right) and projected images of *Il Duce* (the leader) as a 20th-century Caesar who would restore the ancient glories of the mighty Roman empire. Mussolini's power was limited by the strength of the Catholic Church, which he was careful not to attack. Mussolini also sidelined the Italian monarchy rather than abolishing it. Once he had achieved power, Mussolini used little violence to maintain his position. Four thousand anti-fascists were imprisoned and thousands more beaten up, but only ten were actually killed.

Mussolini's attempts to modernize Italy's economy did strengthen industries with military importance, such as the metal and chemical industries. Roads and railroads were improved for

Image of a leader

Both Mussolini and Hitler created images of themselves as the leader and carefully controlled the image that the mass media projected of them. But the style that each chose was very different.

Hitler was usually portrayed as serious, aloof, and distant, almost as a divine figure, staring into a future that only he had the wisdom to foresee. Mussolini, by contrast, played a variety of roles, from warrior, decked out in military uniform, to man of culture, playing the violin, to family man, surrounded by his children. He was even photographed, stripped to the waist, helping peasants gather the harvest. For Hitler this would have been unimaginable. The Italian press was told that Mussolini's name must always be printed in capital letters and they could never print pictures that might contradict his strong man image, such as showing him dancing or talking to a priest.

Stalin, who ordered or organized the deaths of millions, was frequently portrayed as a kindly father figure, surrounded by crowds of adoring small children offering him bouquets of flowers. During the war his image incorporated traditional Russian **patriotism**, such as the shadows of past heroes in the background.

the same reason. Electricity output tripled between 1920 and 1935. Strikes were banned, along with beauty contests and the reporting of crime. Population growth was encouraged so that Italy could have a bigger army. As a result, bachelors were taxed for being single, women were banned from government jobs, and everyone employed by the government, from teachers to postal workers, was ordered to marry or lose their job.

To reestablish Italy as a great imperial power, Mussolini devoted a quarter of all government spending to the armed forces, conquering Ethiopia and sending 50,000 troops to fight for Franco in the Spanish Civil War. These adventures were a terrible waste of resources. When Mussolini disastrously decided to join in World War II, Italy simply could not arm its soldiers and its forces found themselves fighting with tanks, planes, and ships far inferior to their opponents. There were disastrous defeats in the Balkans and North Africa. This created an anti-war group among the military, which overthrew Mussolini in 1943.

As the monarchy still survived, it provided an alternative focus for national loyalty. Italian **partisans** fought on the Allied side against an occupying German army that killed 36,000 of them and shot 10,000 more in **reprisals**. Mussolini was rescued from imprisonment by Nazi special forces and set up a powerless puppet-state, the Republic of Salo, with Nazi backing. Nazi defeat made him flee in disguise. He was caught by communist partisans and shot. The war cost Italy a third of its national wealth and left 300,000 dead.

Nazi Germany

In 1933, Hitler came to power by legal means, at the invitation of the President of Germany's republican government and as leader of the largest single party in the Reichstag (German parliament). He was supported by experienced political and business leaders who hoped to control him for their own ends. Hitler wanted to crush communism and put a powerful Germany at the head of a reorganized Europe. This would be free from Jews, **Slavs**, and other *Untermenschen* (sub-humans), who would be reduced to slavery and eventually wiped out.

Within a month of Hitler's rise to power, the Reichstag burned down. Just how and why was not clear, but it gave Hitler a golden chance to declare a state of emergency and get the members of the

Reichstag to grant him powers to rule by **decree**. The Reichstag itself was soon abolished. Members of the Nazi secret service and armed militias were given police powers. A campaign of *Gleichschaltung* (streamlining) removed everyone the Nazis regarded as enemies—Jews, communists, socialists, and many leaders of trade unions and churches—from the armed forces, law courts, civil service, education system, big business, and media. Hundreds of thousands of writers, teachers, lawyers, scientists, and artists fled abroad. Hundreds of thousands more were arrested and sent to concentration camps, along with gypsies, homosexuals, and beggars. In theory they were there to be reeducated through work and lectures. In practice they were starved, beaten, tortured, or executed.

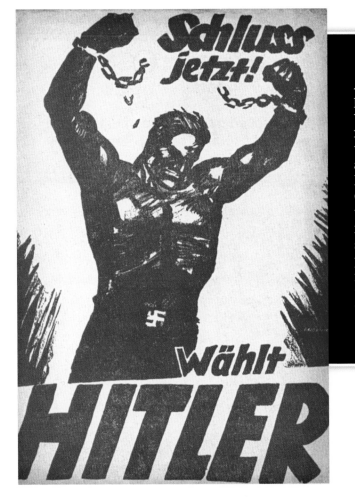

A Nazi election poster claims that a vote for Hitler will free Germany from the chains of despair and humiliation. Hitler's appeal to the German electorate was his promise to restore the nation's shattered pride and put unemployed millions back to work—which he did with speedy success.

The Nazi takeover of Germany was far more rapid and far more complete than the fascist takeover in Italy. It was also far more bloody. There was no monarchy as an alternative focus of loyalty. Divided between Protestant and Catholic, the churches were also much weaker in their opposition. As Germany was much richer and more technologically advanced than Italy, Nazi dictatorship could be much more efficient. Mass-produced radios were installed in every school, railroad station, and public building, so that Hitler could address the entire nation whenever he wanted.

Hitler, unlike Mussolini, equipped his armed forces well. He put Germans back to work, built impressive apartment complexes and *Autobahnen* (highways), and hosted the 1936 Olympics in Berlin to show off the superiority of the Germans as the world's Master Race. Unemployment fell from six million in 1933 to 300,000 by 1939. Nazi supporters were rewarded with homes, businesses, art treasures, and belongings stolen from Jews driven abroad by Nazi persecution. Workers lost the right to free trade unions, but got cheap holidays.

Hitler's goals were summed up in a series of simple slogans. The overriding idea was that the Germans were the world's greatest people. Purged of foreign influences (especially Jewish), and united by a disciplined movement, the nation would march forward to dominate the world. The idea that Germans should be "*Ein Reich, Ein Volk, Ein Führer*" (one state, one people, one leader) led Hitler to demand that Germany's borders should expand to take in all *Auslandsdeutsche*—Germans living under foreign rule. This led to a Nazi takeover of Austria, the border areas of Czechoslovakia and the port of Memel in Lithuania.

In September 1939, World War II began when Hitler invaded Poland with the excuse that he was liberating German-speaking people living under Polish rule. Poland was defeated within weeks. The following spring German armies defeated and occupied Belgium, the Netherlands, Denmark, Norway, and France. The next year they invaded hundreds of miles into the Soviet Union. German defeats began in 1942, but it took three more years to destroy the Nazi regime. While few Italians were prepared to die for fascism and many were glad to fight against it, the hold of the Nazi dictatorship over the German people proved much harder to break.

Crowds and power

Large meetings and rallies have been an important feature of dictatorial **regimes**. They provide a substitute for reasoned argument and an opportunity to play on emotions. Both Hitler and Mussolini were brilliant public speakers, able to whip huge crowds into a frenzy of hatred or adoration. Major rallies were carefully stage-managed and often held at night, so that flaming torches or blazing searchlights could be used for dramatic effect, concentrating all attention on the leader and drowning distractions in darkness. Every September, Nazis from all over Germany gathered at Nuremberg for a huge rally. In 1936 Hitler told them, "Not every one of you sees me and I do not see every one of you. But I feel you and you feel me.... we are with him and he with us, and we are now Germany !"

Hitler explained the power of the large rallies in his book, *Mein Kampf* (My Struggle), "in it the individual, who at first ... feels lonely ... gets the picture of a larger community which in most people has a strengthening, encouraging effect ... the visible ... agreement of thousands confirms to him the rightness of his new belief ... The will, the longing and also the power of thousands are concentrated in every individual."

Hitler arrives at the Berlin Olympic Stadium to address a crowd of 132,000 members of the Hitler Youth organization.

The defeat of Nazism cost Germany three-and-a-half million dead, twelve million refugees, and the division of the country into two separate states for half a century. Both fascist Italy and Nazi Germany promised prosperity, but by aggression in war brought defeat which destroyed their achievements.

Imitators and allies

The inter-war regimes of Hungary under Admiral Horthy (1868–1957), Poland under General Pilsudski (1867–1935), Austria under Chancellor Dollfuss (1892–1934), and Portugal under Antonio Salazar (1889–1970) are better described as **authoritarian** than completely dictatorial. All were fiercely anti–communist, but they permitted a limited degree of political freedom for some parties and newspapers and respected the influence of the Roman Catholic Church. General Franco (1892–1975), commander of the military rebels who had destroyed the Spanish republic in a terrible civil war (1936–39), refused to be drawn into World War II and, free from outside interference, tightened his hold on power. He ruled until his death in 1975 but arranged for the monarchy to be restored under King Juan Carlos I, who swiftly returned Spain to democracy.

During World War II, the Nazis installed fascist figureheads in short-lived puppet-states they created in Slovakia and Croatia. In Romania General Antonescu (1882–1946) drove King Carol into exile, proclaimed himself the nation's *Conducator* (guide) and plunged it into a catastrophic alliance with Germany against the USSR.

What Dictatorships Achieve

The impact of dictatorship varies greatly according to the personality and goals of the dictator and the circumstances he faces. The following examples show a range of possibilities. The first group of dictators can perhaps claim to have had good intentions for their people, the second were simply out for themselves. These examples also show that there is no simple link between a ruler's intentions and their results, or between a country's natural wealth and its people's prosperity. The third section looks at personal governments in the modern Middle East, and asks whether or not they were or still are dictatorships.

Well intended

Mustafa Kemal, Atatürk

What is now the **republic** of Turkey was once the core of the sprawling, multi-ethnic Ottoman Empire. Ruled by a sultan who claimed to be the heir (khalifa, or caliph) of the prophet Muhammad, the empire was based on Islam, but tolerated Christians and Jews.

In World War I, the sultan sided with Germany. Defeat cost the Ottomans most of their territories outside Anatolia and tempted Greece to take more by war. The Greeks were soundly beaten by the Turkish general Mustafa Kemal. Hailed as a hero, Kemal accepted the loss of non-Turkish territories, abolished the Caliphate and made Turkey a republic with himself as president.

Kemal blamed defeat in World War I on the corruption, and incompetence of Ottoman rule. He wanted to remodel the new Turkey on a modern, Western example. This meant expanding and upgrading industry, education, and transportation and changing traditional customs to fit in with European standards, such as abandoning the Islamic calendar and Arabic script. Kemal threw himself completely into his mission, leading by example under the slogan "Be proud you are Turkish."

Because Turks revered Kemal as a patriot, they accepted such dramatic changes as giving women the right to vote and moving the capital to Ankara. All Turks were required to take Western-style family names and Kemal became known as Atatürk—Father of the Turks. Islam was too powerful for Atatürk to abolish, but he tried to keep it out of politics by banning many Islamic organizations and making education purely **secular**. Atatürk's long-term intention was to turn Turkey into a genuine democracy with competing political parties, but in his own lifetime he tolerated little opposition to his reforms. The depth of national mourning at his death showed that Atatürk was genuinely respected for his achievements. His picture still adorns every school, post office, town hall, and public building in Turkey.

The Pahlavi dynasty
Atatürk's example was followed in Iran by Reza Khan (1878–1944), an army officer who overthrew the last shah of the Kajar dynasty, declaring himself shah of a new Pahlavi dynasty. His efforts to Westernize Iran

Mustafa Kemal Atatürk (1881–1938) (left) was like a dictator in the Roman sense, rescuing his country from crisis. He set an example of wearing Western clothing to show Turks what it meant to be modern.

were much less successful, partly because he lacked Atatürk's popular support, partly because the hold of Islam on everyday life was even stronger than in Turkey. His son, Mohammad Reza Shah Pahlavi (1919–1980), pushed Westernization even harder, provoking a backlash which led to his overthrow and the establishment of an Islamic republic in 1979.

Kwame Nkrumah

Kwame Nkrumah (1909–1972) led the British West African **colony** of Gold Coast to independence in 1957 by largely peaceful means, and became its first president. Nkrumah changed the country's name to Ghana, the name of a past great African empire. This was a clue to Nkrumah's long-term goal of bringing together former European colonies in Africa into a new united Africa, under the leadership of Ghana and himself. Nkrumah had spent many years abroad, studying in the United States and Great Britain. He promoted himself as a great thinker and published many books on political questions and the nature of African culture. Many of these were probably written by other people.

By African standards, Ghana was well-off at the time of its independence, thanks to its thriving cocoa industry. Nkrumah used government revenue to build impressive buildings, create new industries, and support prestigious projects like a national airline. Such ventures wasted resources that could have been better spent on improving such services as rural roads and basic healthcare. But Nkrumah wanted results and ignored the fact that most government-supported businesses were inefficient and corrupt. At the same time he traveled widely, determined to show himself as a major international statesman. In the end, his efforts to create pan-African unity led to nothing.

As Nkrumah's government became increasingly dictatorial, he blamed political opponents for its failures. As early as 1958, he introduced a law that allowed suspected enemies to be arrested and imprisoned without trial. The media could only publish stories that made Nkrumah and Ghana look successful. Trade unions, universities, and the courts were brought under government control. In 1964 Nkrumah decreed that there would be only one political party, which he would lead. He decreed that he was now president for life.

Nkrumah (waving) chose to wear the robes of a chief to show respect for African tradition and independence from the West.

In 1966, while Nkrumah was away in Beijing, the Ghanaian military seized power. Ghana was left to struggle out of the mess into which he had led it. Nkrumah's magnificent presidential palace is now a forgotten ruin.

Fidel Castro

After Cuba won its independence from Spain in 1902, the United States came to dominate its economy and often interfered in its politics to protect U.S. interests. Fulgencio Batista was dictator of Cuba from 1952 to 1959. By this time, a few Cubans were very wealthy and most were very poor. Despite its large army, Batista's regime was overthrown by Cuban exile Fidel Castro (born in 1927) whose **guerrilla** force of a few dozen men turned into a tidal wave of discontent. Batista's soldiers and police simply crumbled before it.

Castro's regime confiscated much wealth, including many U.S.-owned businesses, and looked to the USSR as an alternative source of trade, aid, and weapons. Castro announced his conversion to communism and the Soviet Union became the mainstay of the economy. Cuba's prosperity depended almost entirely on sugar, rum, and cigars, which were exported to the USSR and its allies. In return, Cuba sent troops to fight for pro-Soviet movements in countries such as Angola.

Castro's regime stressed health and education for all. As a result Cubans had the highest life expectancy in Latin America (76 years) and a literacy rate of 96 percent, outranking neighboring Jamaica (86 percent) and resource-rich Brazil (84 percent). Sports were also given a high priority as a way of winning international prestige.

On the other hand, Cuba remained a poor country and thousands left in small boats, across shark-infested seas, to seek their fortunes in the United States.

The collapse of the USSR greatly damaged the Cuban economy, forcing it to focus on tourism as an alternative source of income. With the tourists came Western ideas that threatened to undermine Cuba's unique communism.

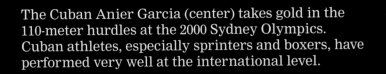

The Cuban Anier Garcia (center) takes gold in the 110-meter hurdles at the 2000 Sydney Olympics. Cuban athletes, especially sprinters and boxers, have performed very well at the international level.

Plunderers

Political scientists have invented the term kleptocracy—rule by thieves—to describe the style of dictatorial government that loots a country of its wealth for the personal benefit of the ruler, his family, and henchmen. Africa, rich in resources but weak in its institutions and starved of skilled political manpower to build them, has provided dramatic examples.

Jean-Bédel Bokassa

Jean-Bédel Bokassa (1921–1996) won numerous bravery awards in the French colonial army before rising rapidly to become chief of staff of the newly independent Central African Republic. He seized power in a coup in 1966. Bokassa not only had opponents killed, but personally took part in the murder of 100 schoolchildren.

For trade reasons, successive French governments supported Bokassa until an embarrassing scandal broke over a diamond given to French President Giscard d'Estaing. After Bokassa physically attacked the

Emperor Bokassa's coronation. After declaring himself president for life, in 1977 Bokassa spent $20 million—a third of his government's annual revenue—on having himself crowned emperor, in imitation of his hero, Napoleon.

French ambassador, French paratroopers overthrew him by force, while pretending that the coup was an internal affair. Bokassa fled to exile, but returned voluntarily in 1986 to serve seven years in prison for the murder of schoolchildren.

Idi Amin
Idi Amin (1925–2003), though barely literate, became a senior officer of the Ugandan army under President Milton Obote (1924–2005), who relied on him to suppress opposition. Obote was about to replace him when Amin struck first. Although he gave the impression of being a rather simple-minded, slightly ridiculous soldier, he removed Obote and then ruled by sheer terror.

In 1972, Uganda's entire Asian business community was expelled, so that the new regime could plunder their property. The Asians were relatively fortunate as an estimated 300,000 native Ugandans died under Amin's rule (1971–1979). He personally murdered dozens of people, including the Anglican archbishop, feeding many of his victims to crocodiles.

The economy fell apart in chaos and Amin's forces eventually collapsed before an invading army of Ugandan exiles, supported by neighboring Tanzania. Amin fled to safety in Libya and then Saudi Arabia.

Joseph Mobutu
Congo, fabulously rich with gold, diamonds, copper, cobalt, oil, and timber, was misruled from 1965 to 1997 by ex-soldier-turned-journalist President Mobutu (1930–97). He was a former general who changed the country's name to Zaire as part of his plan to return the country to a genuinely African culture. For the same reason he changed his own name from Joseph-Désiré Mobutu to Mobutu Sese Seko Kuku Ngbendu Wa Za Banga (which means "the all-powerful warrior who, because of his endurance and inflexible will to win, will go from conquest to conquest, leaving fire in his wake").

The damage Mobutu inflicted was caused more by corruption, neglect, and massive incompetence than by systematic cruelty. Protected by a bodyguard recruited from his own Ngbandi people, Mobutu played on the rivalries of Congo's 250 other ethnic groups to provide excuses for the failures of his rule. By posing as a strong anti-communist, he also gained aid and military support from the United States, France, Belgium, and Israel—but also accepted military advisers from communist China and North Korea.

By the 1980s Mobutu's personal fortune was estimated at $4 billion, not to mention his 20 overseas properties, valued at $37 million. In 1997 he was driven out by his own failing health and a rebel movement supported by democratic South Africa, the United States, and most of Zaire's neighbors. He died in exile.

Hastings Banda
The rule of ex-doctor Hastings Banda (1898–1997) in Malawi was not too bloody and chaotic, though he did have political opponents executed. Scornful of the opinion of other black African leaders, Banda was happy to trade with South Africa and accept aid from its government, even though it oppressed its own black population. Living standards in Malawi rose slowly but steadily as Banda promoted himself from prime minister (1963) to president for life (1971). His own living standards certainly rose, until senility forced him out. His death revealed that he had exported some $320 million to overseas bank accounts.

Nicolae Ceausescu
The nearest the communist world has come to a **kleptocracy** is Romania under the rule of Nicolae Ceausescu (1918–1989). A member of the party's central committee at 27, he took 20 years to become general secretary but then concentrated power in his own hands to become commander-in-chief and head of state as well.

Ceausescu appointed family members to positions of power that they used to enrich themselves. Meanwhile, to pay off Romania's foreign debts, he forced it to export food and oil, causing acute shortages of both at home. In 1983 even TV was rationed to two hours a day, most of it about Ceausescu and his wife, Elena, who were shown as brilliant leaders, adored everywhere they went. He ordered every family to have at least five children, and bulldozed dozens of traditional villages to force people to live in apartment complexes, where they could be controlled more easily. Opposition was crushed by a 100,000-strong

The Ceausescu regime ended on Christmas, 1989. When unarmed protesters were shot down by the Securitate, the army sided with the people and helped the revolt to spread. The dictator and his wife fled, were recaptured, and shot on Christmas Day after a makeshift trial.

These examples are only five of many dictatorial regimes that have made life a misery for millions in recent times. At the time of writing, for example, human rights experts are most concerned with what is happening in Zimbabwe. Here the mass murder and tyrannical government of President Mugabe have reduced a once prosperous country to one of the poorest in Africa.

Middle East Dictators

The Middle East has always given problems to students of dictatorship in modern times. At first glance, the region seemed overrun with dictators, from Saddam Hussein in Iraq, to President Mubarak of Egypt, and the kings and princes of Saudi Arabia, Jordan, Kuwait, and elsewhere. A closer look, however, suggests that Middle Eastern dictatorship was not always quite what it seemed.

Two factors limited the power of the region's non-democratic rulers: tradition and religion. Like the medieval kings of Europe, rulers of the Middle East who inherited their power were expected to abide by their society's traditions. Men like King Abdullah of Saudi Arabia, the al-Sabah rulers of Kuwait, the al-Khalifahs of Bahrain, and Sultan ali Abdallah Saleh of Oman believed they had a duty to consult with their families and with important members of the community when they made important policy decisions. In theory, they had the power to do what they wanted, like a Hitler or a Stalin; in practice, they could not afford to alienate powerful interests. King Faisal of Saudi Arabia (1903–1975) held the *majlis* (public consultation) to find out what his people wanted. He was assassinated by a member of his own family at one of these majlis.

Islam was another powerful force limiting the power of would-be dictators in the Middle East. However much King Faisal of Saudi Arabia wanted his country to adopt the technology of the 20th century, he had to take into account the views of the country's

47

religious leaders. He even faced serious rioting when he allowed the country's first TV station to open in 1965. Moreover, although Islam says little directly or indirectly about democracy, it does make it clear that rulers have a holy duty to care for their subjects' welfare. Such an attitude is hardly conducive to dictatorship.

It is not surprising, therefore, that the Middle Eastern rulers who in recent times were most dictatorial did not come from the traditional ruling class and did not pay much attention to religion. Syria's dictator-president Hafez al-Assad (1930–2000) was a poor soldier who made his way to the top by ruthless determination. Iraq's Saddam Hussein followed a similar path. President Hosni Mubarak (1928–) was a bright student who climbed to power via the Egyptian air force. Neither Assad, Hussein, nor Mubarak, all of whom might well be considered dictators, showed much interest in their countries' Islamic heritage. Indeed, all three came into conflict with religious leaders, whose influence they saw as undermining their own.

The end of a dictator. Egyptian soldiers, some in shock, some attending to the wounded, on the platform where President Sadat had just been assassinated, 1981.

How Dictatorships End

Searching for stability

Atatürk's Turkey and Mexico after the revolution of 1910–1920 did grow into democracies. In 20th-century Spain, Greece, Chile, Argentina, and Brazil, democracy was successfully restored after periods of dictatorial or military rule. In Nigeria, Pakistan, Thailand, and Peru, the military have repeatedly intervened in politics, leading to periods of strong-man rule by generals. However, their armed forces have also repeatedly shown a willingness to go back to their barracks and turn the problems of running the country back to civilian politicians.

Communist collapses

The breakup of the Soviet Union in 1990–1991 enabled the populations of its former allies in eastern Europe to overthrow their own communist governments through mass demonstrations. Poland was already well on the way to democracy thanks to its Solidarity movement, based on its trade-unions. In East Germany and Czechoslovakia, the transition was almost bloodless, in Romania it was violent. The end of the Cold War made the United States much less willing to maintain links with dictatorial governments because they claimed to be strongly anti-communist. This, and increasing public anger in Western democracies at human rights abuses, has made it harder for dictatorships to benefit from trade and contacts with democratic countries and the global corporations based in them. One result of this has been the general disappearance of dictatorships in Latin America since the 1980s.

Death and disorder

As in the world of ancient Greece, the simple fact of the death of the dictator can be enough to end his regime, though this can be the prelude to chaos rather than freedom and stability.

Yugoslavia's wartime guerrilla leader Marshal Tito (1892–1980) managed to create a communist state that was fiercely independent of the USSR. He also controlled the tensions between the country's different nationalities. Tito left behind a leadership team that maintained this stability for a decade, until old rivalries between Serbs, Croats, and Bosnians led to disastrous wars of partition and the emergence of authoritarian regimes under Slobodan Milosevic in Serbia and Franjo Tudjman in Croatia. In neighboring Albania, the death of Enver Hoxha in 1985 brought to an end 40 years of communist dictatorship that left the country the poorest in Europe, and led to a decline into general criminality which threatens the stability of its Balkan neighbors.

Family ties

Perhaps remarkably, family loyalties can still prove as important in some 20th-century states as they were in medieval kingdoms, where sons followed fathers onto the throne.

On the poor Caribbean island of Haiti, François "Papa Doc" Duvalier ruled from 1957 to 1971 by a mixture of corruption and terror. He gained support from the rural black poor against the traditionally

In regimes dominated by a single leader, a funeral offers the opportunity to show loyalty. Here Bashar al-Assad (facing camera with raised fist, left), successor and son of Hafez al-Assad as ruler of Syria, accompanies his father's coffin.

powerful *mulatto* (mixed race) elite of the towns. He even managed to pass on his position to his teenage son, Jean-Claude "Baby Doc" Duvalier, who was not overthrown until 1986. Despite U.S. attempts to stabilize Haiti, by using troops to guarantee order and by supervising fair elections, Haiti has remained prone to political violence.

North Korea is the only remaining state to cling to the hard-line communism of Stalin's day. The dictator Kim Il-Sung (known as the Great Leader), ruled from 1948 to 1994 and managed to pass his position on to his son Kim Jong-Il (known as the Dear Leader), who has ruled ever since, despite the fact that the country's massive spending on weapons has impoverished it and brought widespread famine.

The cult of personality

Concentrating power in the hands of a single individual has led to the emergence of a cult of personality in both fascist and communist regimes. Concentrating loyalty on a personality not only increased their power, but distracted attention from gaps or contradictions in their political plans. As long as the leader wields power everything is, by definition, under control. At its most extreme, the cult of personality presents the leader as a universal genius, worthy not just of obedience but of adoration and the highest sacrifice. Members of the Hitler Youth were required to swear, "to devote all my energies and my strength to the savior of our country, Adolf Hitler. I am willing and ready to give up my life for him, so help me God." Although Stalin himself was largely responsible for the disastrous defeats suffered by the Soviet army at the hands of German invaders, Soviet propaganda hailed him as a military genius.

Perhaps the most extreme personality cult was built up around the North Korean communist leaders, Kim Il Sung (1912–1994) and his son and successor Kim Jong-Il (1941–). The country's media refer to the latter as, "The peerless commander, heaven on earth and saviour of the Korean people." In February 2002 Kim Jong-Il's sixtieth birthday was marked by an inscription in his honor carved onto a mountainside in letters 100 feet high.

Intervention and isolation

Officially Libya has a People's Government, which claims to have abolished its institutions, such as its police force and law courts, and replaced them with committees of ordinary citizens. In practice, the country is controlled by Colonel Muammar al-Qaddafi, who has ruled since he overthrew the monarchy in 1969. As well as keeping a tight hold over his own country, the eccentric Qaddafi supported terrorism around the world with money, training, weapons, and explosives. Those who suffered included neighboring Egypt and Sudan, as well as the United States, Great Britain, and France. The United States responded in 1986 with an air strike intended to kill Qaddafi, and strongly supported UN **sanctions** on Libya. Oil wealth enabled the country to survive international isolation until the early 21st century, when Qaddafi, worried that the United States might attack him in earnest after the 9/11 terrorist attacks, suddenly changed course and made peace with the West. He admitted to having possessed chemical and other illegal weapons, and guaranteed that he had destroyed them.

Iraq's Saddam Hussein had no such change of heart. Initially the friend of the West when he fought Iran (1980–88), the ruthless dictator lost all friends when he invaded Kuwait in 1990. After defeat in the First Gulf War (1991), he was isolated by UN sanctions and subjected to periodic attacks from the U.S. and Great Britain. Like Qaddafi, Hussein had developed illegal weapons of mass destruction and made life as difficult as he could for the UN inspection teams sent to check whether he was destroying them. The Iraqi dictator, whose evil regime had been responsible for the cruel deaths of thousands of his fellow countrypeople, was finally overthrown in 2003 when a U.S.-led coalition force invaded Iraq and installed a democratic government friendly to the West. Hussein was tried in an Iraqi court, found guilty of crimes against humanity, and sentenced to death. The sentence was carried out in December 2006.

In 1975 Pol Pot (1925–1998), a founder of the local communist party, seized power in Cambodia with the backing of a guerrilla army of peasants, known as the Khmer Rouge. The country had been badly affected by the lingering effects of war in neighboring Vietnam, which had killed 150,000 Cambodians and made two million homeless. Pol Pot's answer was to cut all contacts with the outside world and make Cambodia self-supporting by forcing city dwellers to work on the land.

"Look on my works, ye mighty, and despair." Joyful Iraqis mock the beheaded statue of their fallen tyrant, Saddam Hussein, in 2003.

His Khmer Rouge government banned money, religion, foreign languages, newspapers, radio, TV and even bicycles. Two million people, a quarter of the population, were killed or died of starvation before Pol Pot was overthrown by a Vietnamese invasion in 1979. Pol Pot led Khmer Rouge guerilla resistance to Cambodia's new Vietnamese-backed government for another 17 years. He finally lost control of the Khmer Rouge and was arrested by them, but he died of natural causes before he could be tried for his crimes.

Can dictatorships survive?

There have always been dictators of one kind or another, and there always will be. In the West it is fashionable to think, after the collapse of Soviet communism, that democracy will gradually spread over the whole world. However, democracy is a frail flower that takes years to take root and is rarely strong enough to withstand major difficulties such as defeat in war or economic recession. It is worth remembering, for instance, that Hitler and Mussolini, two of the 20th century's most famous dictators, both first came to power by democratic means. Dictatorship may be on the decline at the moment, but we can be sure that whenever things start to go seriously wrong in a country, there is bound to be a power-hungry individual ready to put himself forward as a savior. So a new dictatorship will be born.

So, What Is Dictatorship?

Dictatorship was known to the ancient Greeks, but only became prominent as a form of government after Napoleon. Modern dictatorship is distinguished by its ruthless use of force and its concern to mobilize active support for its efforts to change society. The existence of strong alternative institutions, such as a monarchy, army, or church, has tended to limit the changes a dictatorship can make. When a dictatorship succeeds in neutralizing or destroying such institutions, its potential for the abuse of power is greatly increased.

The most extreme dictatorships have brought disaster on their countries. Adolf Hitler tried to rid the world of communism but instead ensured that half of Europe, including half of Germany itself, would be ruled by communists for half a century. The 1959 census figures for the USSR make it possible to calculate that, thanks to Stalin's persecutions in the 1930s, its population was 20 percent smaller than it would otherwise have been. In 1958 Mao Zedong called on China to make a Great Leap Forward and create modern industries overnight. The result was failed harvests and mass-starvation. In 1966 he launched a Cultural Revolution to restore his personal leadership of the party. Led by fanatical young Red Guards, mobs attacked figures in authority, such as party officials, factory managers, and teachers. Millions of people died, and the country's education system and industry were set back years.

Interestingly, 21st-century communications make it more difficult for modern dictators to exercise the sort of power once wielded by those of the previous century. As the current Chinese regime has realized, Internet information is free, universal, and almost beyond control—and if dictators cannot control information, they cannot control people. So although dictatorship will always be with us, there is a chance that over the years it will become harder to establish. Therein lies hope for a better future …

Timeline

138–78 BCE	Sulla, Roman dictator
c.102–44 BCE	Julius Caesar, Roman dictator
1513	Niccolo Machiavelli of Florence publishes *The Prince*, a handbook for ruthless rulers
1653–58	Oliver Cromwell rules Britain as Lord Protector
1804–15	Napoleon rules France as emperor
1819–25	Simon Bolivar liberates former Spanish colonies of South America
1852–70	Napoleon III rules a Second Empire in France
1914–18	World War I
1917	Communist revolution overthrows royal rule in Russia
1922	Mussolini's March on Rome
1923	General Primo de Rivera seizes power in Spain General Mustafa Kemal declares Turkey a republic
1928	Stalin becomes unopposed ruler of the Soviet Union
1933	Hitler comes to power in Germany
1936–39	Francisco Franco wins civil war in Spain to become *Caudillo*
1945	Fascist regime overthrown in Germany
1949	George Orwell publishes *Nineteen Eighty-Four*
1959	Fidel Castro overthrows Fulgencio Batista in Cuba
1962	Military takeover in Burma
1966	General Suharto overthrows Ahmed Sukarno in Indonesia Kwame Nkrumah overthrown by a military coup in Ghana
1969	Colonel Muammar Qaddafi overthrows the monarchy in Libya
1973	General Pinochet seizes power in Chile
1975	Spain restored to democracy by King Juan Carlos I
1977	General Zia ul-Haq overthrows civilian rule of Zulfikar Ali Bhutto in Pakistan Jean-Bedel Bokassa of the Central African Republic crowns himself emperor
1979	Ayatollah Ruhollah Khomeini leads an Islamic Revolution in Iran

	Idi Amin flees from Uganda
	Saddam Hussein becomes undisputed dictator of Iraq
1985	Collapse of communist dictatorship in Albania with death of Enver Hoxha
1986	"Baby Doc" Duvalier overthrown in Haiti
1986	Robert Mugabe changes Zimbabwe's constitution to become its executive president
1989	Hundreds killed as Chinese troops open fire on pro-democracy demonstrators in Beijing's Tiananmen Square
1989–91	Breakup of the Soviet Union
1991	Overthrow of Colonel Mengistu in Ethiopia
1999	General Pervez Musharraf takes power in Pakistan
2001	Slobodan Milosevic charged with war crimes and crimes against humanity at an international tribunal in The Hague
2002	Hu Jintao replaces Jiang Zemin as China's premier Libya's President Qaddafi decides to cooperate with the world community
2003	U.S.-led invasion of Iraq to remove President Saddam Hussein
2005	Saudi Arabia allows local elections UN declares that President Mugabe, Zimbabwe's dictator, has reduced the country to "meltdown"
2006	President Castro becomes seriously ill. His brother may need to take over leadership of Cuba North Korea tests a nuclear device Saddam Hussein is found guilty of crimes against humanity and executed

Further Information

Further reading

Anderson, Dale. *Saddam Hussein.* Minneapolis, Minn.: Lerner, 2004.

Faulkner, Anne. *Mao Zedong: 20th Century History Makers.* New York: Franklin Watts, 2003.

Lee, Stephen J. *European Dictatorships, 1918–1945.* New York: Routledge, 2003.

Shields, Charles J. *Saddam Hussein.* Broomall, Penn.: Chelsea House Publishers, 2002.

Taylor, David. *Leading Lives: Adolf Hitler.* Chicago, Ill.: Heinemann Library, 2002.

Thorne, James. *Julius Caesar: Conqueror and Dictator.* New York: Rosen Publishing Group, 2002.

Wallechinsky, David. *Tyrants: The World's 20 Worst Living Dictators.* New York: Regan Books, 2006.

Websites

There are dozens of websites devoted to the world's dictators. Here are a few places to start:

http://library.thinkquest.org/19092
www.history1900s.about.com/cs/idiamin/index.htm
www.thedictatorship.com
www.time.com/time/time100/leaders/profile/mao

And here are some of the better specific websites:

www.spartacus.schoolnet.co.uk/COLDmao.htm
www.history.com/encyclopedia.do?articleId = 209062

Some 20th-Century Dictators

Mao Zedong (1893–1976) Founder of Communist China
Born a farmer's son, Mao became active in student politics, founding the Chinese Communist Party in 1921. Mao adapted communist theory to suit the needs of Chinese peasants, setting up a peasant-led commune at Jiangxi in 1931–34. When Chinese Nationalists attacked it, he led 100,000 followers on a 6,000-mile (9,700-kilometer) Long March (1934–36) to the safety of Yenan. Two-thirds of the marchers died but from there Mao led guerrilla resistance to Japanese invasion and later defeated the Nationalists, declaring China an independent communist state in 1949. Mao ordered the disastrous Great Leap Forward (1958–60) and the hugely destructive Cultural Revolution (1966–69). He was an accomplished poet, and his political writings were regarded as works of genius by the fanatical young Red Guards who did his bidding. Despite his responsibility for up to 20 million deaths, Mao is still honored for ending years of foreign interference in China.

Juan Péron (1895–1974) Dictator of Argentina 1946–55
Handsome, charming, a champion skier and fencer, Péron was a professional army officer who had lived in and admired Mussolini's Italy. As one of the military who seized power in Argentina in 1943, Péron built a personal following among trade unions there, which enabled him to become president in 1946. He was a brilliant public speaker but gained even more popularity through his glamorous wife, Evita (1919–52), a minor actress with a genius for publicizing her charity work. Péron's attacks on foreign-owned businesses were as popular as his welfare reforms and support for local industry. Péron and Evita were genuinely adored by the poor and her sudden early death from cancer plunged the nation into grief. Péron then lost his touch with the people, angered the powerful Catholic Church and army, brought the economy to ruin and was driven into exile. Support for Péronism survived, however, and in 1973 Péron returned in triumph. However, he failed to solve Argentina's continuing problems, and died after a year. His third wife, Isabelita (1931–), took over but was overthrown by the army in 1976.

Ahmed Sukarno (1902–70) President of Indonesia 1945–67
A member of the anti-Dutch movement for Indonesian independence
from its earliest days in the 1920s, Sukarno had an outstanding gift for
languages and could move a group of people to tears or frenzy in any
of a dozen tongues. His great gift to his country was the creation of the
modern Indonesian language, which united a nation of island-dwellers
scattered over 3,000 miles (5,000 kilometers). As first president of an
independent Indonesia, Sukarno's vanity led him to parade as a world
statesman and waste Indonesia's natural wealth on grand projects that
did nothing for the poor. Accused of corruption, he was overthrown by
General Suharto (1921–), whose long period of military rule was even
more corrupt, on an even greater scale. Suharto was driven into exile
by a popular uprising in 1998.

Augusto Pinochet (1915–2006) Dictator of Chile 1973–90
A professional army officer, Pinochet led the military to overthrow the
legally elected government of Salvador Allende, whose reforms for
the poor were blamed for hurting business. Pinochet's government
imprisoned, tortured, and murdered opponents and made life hard for the
poor, but brought Chile prosperity. Pinochet himself passed power back to
an elected president, but he kept his rank as army commander-in-chief,
with immunity from the law for actions committed during his rule.

Slobodan Milosevic (1941–2006)
After a successful career as a communist official, in 1988 Milosevic
became president of Serbia, the most powerful part of Yugoslavia.
His pro-Serb actions made him popular in Serbia but led Slovenia
and Croatia to fight successfully for their independence. Milosevic
encouraged Serb fighters in Bosnia to add lands under their control
to Serbia and then used Serb forces against the Albanian inhabitants
of Kosovo, causing thousands more deaths and a massive refugee
crisis. Within Serbia he and his family abused their position to enrich
themselves and used bribery, violence, and rigged elections to stay
in power. Milosevic was eventually overthrown and handed over to an
international court at The Hague in the Netherlands, to be tried for
crimes against humanity. In 2006 he suffered a heart attack and was
found dead in his cell.

Glossary

arbitrary acting on personal wishes, regardless of law or reason

authoritarian system of government that demands strict obedience, but does not try to control everything

caudillismo tradition of rule by a single dictator in Spanish-speaking countries

charismatic having extraordinary powers of personality

civilian person who is not a member of the army or police force

colony country ruled by another one

communism belief in a government based on the idea that a single ruling political party can run a country for the benefit of all its people better than if they are left to make their own decisions and keep their own private homes, land, and businesses

constitution set of rules setting out how a system of government should work

decree statement having the force of law

democracy system of government by the entire population. Voters usually elect representatives who govern the country.

demonstration parade or mass-meeting in support of a cause

despot absolute ruler or tyrant

dictatorship rule by a single person or small group with complete power, not answerable to a parliament

exile living in another country for political reasons

fascism system of dictatorship that puts the nation before the individual and forbids opposition

guerrilla member of a small armed group, fighting against a larger, regular army

ideology organized system of ideas to be put into practice through political action

junta Spanish word for a group of military officers who have seized power by force

kleptocracy when a ruler uses his power to steal his country's resources

legitimacy having the right to rule

literacy ability to read or write

massacre systematic killing of large numbers of people

militia part-time armed force of volunteers

monarchy system of government in which a country is ruled by a king or queen

Nazi short name of the National Socialist German Workers' Party (Nationalsozialistiche Deutsche Arbeiterpartei), led by Adolf Hitler. The Nazis ruled Germany from 1933–45. Nazism is the German form of fascism.

pagan believer in pre-Christian gods

partisan armed volunteer fighter who is not part of a regular, professional army

patriot person who loves his or her country

post-colonial independent state that was once a colony

propaganda communication through messages and symbols that tries to persuade people to support a particular point of view, usually through appealing to emotion rather than reason

regime system or style of government

reprisals actions taken to punish attacks

republic country in which power is held by the people, or by their elected representatives, not by a monarch. A republic often has an elected president as head of state.

rule of law situation in which citizens are treated fairly, according to known rules applied equally to all

SA (Sturmabteilung) storm troopers: the Nazi Party militia

SS (Schutzstaffel) defense squadron: Hitler's personal bodyguard. The SS eventually grew into a Nazi party army with hundreds of thousands of members.

sanctions limits on trade or other contacts to punish a country

secret police police, usually in civilian clothes, who operate in secret and outside the control of the law and court system, often using threats, torture, and murder

secular non-religious

Slav person speaking one of the Slavonic languages such as Russian, Polish, or Bulgarian

socialist person who believes in using government to make the lives of citizens more equal

Soviet Union Union of Soviet Socialist Republics (USSR), a communist empire governed by Russia that lasted from 1922 to 1991

technocrat person with special skills of management who is especially effective at running large organizations

totalitarian type of dictatorship that tries for complete control over every aspect of people's lives

tyranny rule by an oppressive or cruel ruler, called a tyrant

Index